Christian Jr./Sr High School
2100 Greenfield Dr.
El Cajon, CA 92019

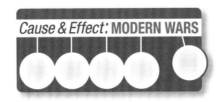

Cause & Effect: MODERN WARS

Cause & Effect: The Persian Gulf War

Tom Streissguth

ReferencePoint Press®

San Diego, CA

© 2018 ReferencePoint Press, Inc.
Printed in the United States

For more information, contact:
ReferencePoint Press, Inc.
PO Box 27779
San Diego, CA 92198
www.ReferencePointPress.com

LIBRARY OF CONGRESS CATALOGING-IN-PUBLICATION DATA

Name: Streissguth, Tom, author
Title: Cause & Effect: The Persian Gulf War/by Tom Streissguth.
Other titles: Cause & Effect | Persian Gulf War
Description: San Diego, CA : ReferencePoint Press, Inc., 2018. | Series:
 Cause & Effect: Modern Wars series | Includes bibliographical references
 and index.
Identifiers: LCCN 2016056739 (print) | LCCN 2016058108 (ebook) | ISBN
 9781682821664 (hardback) | ISBN 9781682821671 (eBook)
Subjects: LCSH: Persian Gulf War, 1991. | Persian Gulf War, 1991--Causes. |
 Persian Gulf War, 1991--United States.
Classification: LCC DS79.72 .S77 2018 (print) | LCC DS79.72 (ebook) | DDC
 956.7044/2--dc23
LC record available at https://lccn.loc.gov/2016056739

CONTENTS

"History is a complex study of the many causes that have influenced happenings of the past and the complicated effects of those varied causes."

—William & Mary School of Education,
Center for Gifted Education

Understanding the causes and effects of historical events, including those that occur within the context of war, is rarely simple. The Cold War's Cuban Missile Crisis, for instance, resulted from a complicated—and at times convoluted—series of events set in motion by US, Soviet, and Cuban actions. And that crisis, in turn, shaped interactions between the United States and the former Soviet Union for years to come. Had any of these events not taken place or had they occurred under different circumstances, the effects might have been something else altogether.

The value of analyzing cause and effect in the context of modern wars, therefore, is not necessarily to identify a single cause for a singular event. The real value lies in gaining a greater understanding of history as a whole and being able to recognize the many factors that give shape and direction to historic events. As outlined by the National Center for History in the Schools at the University of California–Los Angeles, these factors include "the importance of the individual in history . . . the influence of ideas, human interests, and beliefs; and . . . the role of chance, the accidental and the irrational."

ReferencePoint's Cause & Effect: Modern Wars series examines wars of the modern age by focusing on specific causes and consequences. For instance, in *Cause & Effect (Modern Wars): The Cold War,* a chapter explores whether the US military buildup in the 1980s helped end the Cold War. And in *Cause & Effect (Modern Wars): The Vietnam War,* one chapter delves into this question: "How Did Fear of Communism Lead to US Intervention in Vietnam?" Every book in the series includes thoughtful discussion of questions like these— supported by facts, examples, and a mix of fully documented primary and secondary source quotes. Each title also includes an overview of the event so that readers have a broad context for understanding the more detailed discussions of specific causes and their effects.

The value of such study is not limited to the classroom; it can also be applied to many areas of contemporary life. The ability to analyze and interpret history's causes and consequences is a form of critical thinking. Critical thinking is crucial in many professions, ranging from law enforcement to science. Critical thinking is also essential for developing an educated citizenry that fully understands the rights and obligations of living in a free society. The ability to sift through and analyze complex processes and events and identify their possible outcomes enables people in that society to make important decisions.

The Cause & Effect: Modern Wars series has two primary goals. One is to help students think more critically about history and develop a true understanding of its complexities. The other is to help build a foundation for those students to become fully participating members of the society in which they live.

IMPORTANT EVENTS OF THE PERSIAN GULF WAR

August 6
The United Nations (UN) adopts Resolution 661, imposing an international embargo on trade with Iraq.

August 9
US forces begin arriving in northern Saudi Arabia to prepare for military action against Iraq.

July 22
Iraq begins moving military forces to the Kuwait border.

1990 | Jul | Aug | Sept | Oct | Nov

August 2
Iraq invades Kuwait, facing minimal resistance as it gains control of the capital, Kuwait City.

September 14
Britain and France begin deploying troops to the Persian Gulf.

November 29
UN Resolution 678 authorizes use of all means necessary to eject Iraq from Kuwait.

August 5
At a press conference, President George H.W. Bush declares his intention to end Iraq's occupation of Kuwait.

August 8
Iraq annexes Kuwait; Iraqi leader Saddam Hussein declares Kuwait to be his country's nineteenth province.

January 17
The air war phase—nicknamed Operation Desert Storm—begins with heavy bombing of Baghdad and military installations in southern Iraq.

January 12
The US Congress formally authorizes the use of force to liberate Kuwait.

January 22
Iraqi forces begin destruction of oil wells in Kuwait.

March 3
US general Norman Schwarzkopf meets with Iraqi leaders at Safwan, Saudi Arabia, to set peace terms.

| 1991 | Jan | Feb | Mar | Apr | May |

January 18
Iraq begins firing Scud missiles at Israel and Saudi Arabia, causing extensive damage and some civilian casualties.

February 28
After one hundred hours of ground fighting, the United States declares a cease-fire.

February 24
The ground attack, code-named Operation Desert Sabre, begins, with US and coalition forces driving into Kuwait and southern Iraq.

Freedom, War, and Oil

Historians know the flat and fertile lands along the Tigris and Euphrates Rivers as Mesopotamia—the "Land Between the Rivers." This area gave rise to one of the earliest urban civilizations. More than five thousand years ago, the people who lived here built city-states, developed writing and alphabets, and domesticated useful animals. During the twentieth century Mesopotamia became part of the modern nation of Iraq and, in the summer of 1990, it became the cradle of the Persian Gulf War.

This brief conflict lasted just seven months. It began in August 1990 with Iraq's invasion of Kuwait, a small but wealthy emirate (state ruled by an emir, an Arabaic term for monarch) on the Persian Gulf. The United States saw this as a serious threat to its supply of oil from Kuwait and neighboring Saudi Arabia—and to US economic interests—and assembled a coalition of nations whose objective was to end the occupation.

The United States had not been involved in a major military conflict since the Vietnam War. A retreat from Vietnam in 1974 had saddled American military planners with the so-called Vietnam syndrome, which was a reluctance to involve US forces in foreign conflicts. To avoid a similar debacle, the coalition nations deployed a well-trained, well-supplied force of five hundred thousand troops. "From the standpoint of the U.S. Air Force vs. the Iraqi Air Force," commented Representative Bill Alexander of Arkansas, "it's like the New York Giants vs. the Little Sisters of the Poor [a Catholic religious order]."[1] The US-led coalition carried out an air assault lasting five weeks and then invaded Kuwait and Iraq. The ground attack lasted just one hundred hours before the US declared victory, and a cease-fire, in February 1991.

The Aftermath

Although Kuwait won its freedom from Iraqi occupation, the cost was high. Before retreating, the Iraqi military had sabotaged the country's oil-producing infrastructure, including oil wells, refineries, pipelines, and port facilities. Kuwaitis who fled the country returned to find their homes damaged and businesses looted.

In Iraq, the six weeks of bombing and ground conflict wreaked havoc. The coalition deliberately targeted Iraq's transportation and manufacturing infrastructure to undermine support among the Iraqi people for the war. Bombs and missiles destroyed electric power stations, airports, highways, bridges, factories, and railroads while also inflicting damage on city streets, homes, hospitals, and schools.

The defeat also plunged Iraq into a brief civil war. Shiite Muslims in southern Iraq, and Kurds in the north, rose up against Saddam Hussein, the country's president. They hoped to overthrow his government in its time of defeat. Saddam Hussein's air and ground forces put down the revolt, leaving behind massive civilian casualties. The Iraqi leader also used chemical weapons to achieve victory and punish the rebels.

> "What is at stake is more than one small country; it is a big idea: a new world order, where diverse nations are drawn together in common cause to achieve the universal aspirations of mankind—peace and security, freedom, and the rule of law."[2]
>
> —President George H.W. Bush

A New World Order?

Both sides of the Persian Gulf conflict saw themselves as fighting for right and against evil. Kuwait considered itself to be an independent nation. Saddam Hussein, however, viewed Kuwait as an Iraqi province; he declared that his nation had a historic claim to Kuwait. The United States saw Iraq's invasion as an unjustified and illegal action, one that had to be turned back on the principle that stronger nations should not be allowed to seize weaker nations by force. On January 16, 1991, President George H.W. Bush gave a speech before the US Congress in which he declared, "What is at stake is more than one small country; it is a big idea: a new world order, where diverse nations are drawn together in common cause to achieve the universal aspirations of mankind—peace and security, freedom, and the rule of law."[2]

But the United States had another, equally important motive: protecting its access to oil from the Middle East. Kuwait was a major oil

US soldiers prepare for live-fire exercises in the Kuwaiti desert south of the Iraqi border in 2002. Although coalition forces were victorious in the 1991 Persian Gulf War, long-term peace and the security of smaller nations in the Middle East was not achieved.

producer, as was Saudi Arabia—and both countries shared a border with Iraq. Saudi Arabia saw the Iraqi army presence in Kuwait as a direct threat to its oil-producing regions. So did the Americans. Control of the Saudi oil supply by Iraq could drive up prices and cause a global economic crisis.

In view of this threat, US leaders felt they needed to act. But they were also aware of Arab sensitivity to the presence of Western powers on their land. Arab nations had long harbored anger over what they viewed as Western exploitation of their oil resources. For this reason, the United States did not want to act alone; instead, it persuaded Arab countries such as Morocco, Saudi Arabia, and Egypt to join an international coalition to oust the Iraqi army from Kuwait. Coalition building required skill, patience, and time, as the interests of dozens of nations did not necessarily align with those of the United States. In addition, the United States and the Soviet Union—the world's two superpowers—had to overcome decades of mistrust and conflict in order to work together.

Unforeseeable Consequences

The United States was successful in its goal. With Saudi Arabia as a base, the US-led coalition staged a massive invasion of Iraq, defeating the Iraqi army and liberating Kuwait. President Bush and many others praised the outcome as a much-needed boost to America's prestige around the world. "By God, we've kicked the Vietnam syndrome once and for all,"[3] declared Bush.

But the war also had long-term results that were hard to foresee. Victory in the Persian Gulf War brought no permanent answer to the issue of a secure foreign oil supply for the United States or other nations. Nor did it lead, as promised, to a new world order of security for smaller nations. Iraq remained in turmoil, with two of its ethnic and religious minorities, the Shiites and Kurds, pressing for independence.

The use of Saudi Arabia as a base to attack Iraq also had consequences. As the homeland of Muhammad, the founder of Islam, Saudi Arabia was considered by Muslims around the world as holy territory. The presence of US troops on Saudi soil inspired a Saudi citizen, Osama bin Laden, to establish a global terrorist network known as al Qaeda. For Bin Laden and other Muslims, the American alliance with the Saudi government was a religious desecration—one to be fought with violence. After al Qaeda mounted a terrorist attack that killed three thousand Americans on September 11, 2001, the United States saw fit to return to Iraq in 2003 for a much longer and less conclusive war.

A relatively young nation, the United States had yet to learn an important lesson—the conflicts of the Middle East go back a very long time and involve more than a simple struggle for good or evil, for freedom, or for the control of natural resources. Instead, dozens of nations, cultures, political parties, and religious factions are engaged in a constant struggle and negotiation for influence. The presence of foreign powers, and foreign armies, never solves or simplifies these centuries-old conflicts.

CHAPTER ONE

A Brief History of the Persian Gulf War

Shortly after midnight on August 2, 1990, the million-strong army of Iraq invaded Kuwait. Kuwait's army, numbering just twenty thousand men, could offer little resistance. Within a few hours, the Iraqis were storming through the streets of Kuwait City, the capital, and besieging the Dasman Palace, the home of Kuwait's ruling family.

Iraq had been building up its forces along the Kuwait border for two weeks. Many leaders in the United States and Saudi Arabia believed Iraq's leader, Saddam Hussein, was simply threatening Kuwait while also demanding the Kuwaitis slow their production of oil. This would raise the price and help Iraq, another oil-rich country—but one with serious economic problems.

The UN Reacts

The buildup proved to be no bluff. Within twenty-four hours of storming across the border, the Iraqi army was in total control of Kuwait. Iraqi troops looted Kuwaiti banks and businesses and summarily executed civilians found resisting the invasion. But the Iraqis missed their primary target: Kuwait's emir (ruler) and other members of the royal family, most of whom escaped to Saudi Arabia.

On August 3 the United Nations (UN) summoned an emergency meeting of the Security Council. This fifteen-member council debates and votes on resolutions during international emergencies. By a unanimous vote, the council passed Resolution 660, condemning the invasion and calling for Iraq's immediate withdrawal from Kuwait. Two days later, in Washington, DC, President George H.W. Bush announced, "I'm not going to discuss what we're doing in terms of moving of forces. . . . But I view it very seriously, not just that but any threat to any other countries, as well as I view very seriously our determination to reverse out this aggression. . . . This will not stand. This will not stand, this aggression against Kuwait."[4]

Bush and his advisers feared that Saddam Hussein might not stop his army in Kuwait. By moving his forces south, the Iraqi leader was also threatening Saudi Arabia, a US ally and the source of nearly a quarter of the world's crude oil. Although the Saudi military had sophisticated weaponry, much of it purchased from the United States, its army and air force were far smaller than that of Iraq, which boasted the fourth-largest army in the world. Gaining control of the Saudi oil fields, not far from the Iraq border, would allow Saddam Hussein to dictate the terms of any peace agreement.

> "This will not stand. This will not stand, this aggression against Kuwait."[4]
>
> —President George H.W. Bush

To meet this threat, the United States sent a team of diplomats to Saudi Arabia. Their task was to convince Saudi leaders to allow the United States to station troops, tanks, artillery, and aircraft on Saudi territory. Building forward bases near the Iraq border would not only defend Saudi Arabia and its oil fields but also would allow for a ground offensive into Kuwait and southern Iraq.

Problems of History

The history of the Middle East complicated the mission. Saudi Arabia was home to important ancient Islamic shrines, and many Muslims would see a Western military presence on Saudi territory as a desecration of holy territory by infidels (nonbelievers). Among many Arabs, Westerners were also seen as hostile outsiders intent on controlling valuable oil resources. The United States would have to tread carefully while persuading nations in the region to join a coalition against Iraq.

Colonialism also posed a thorny issue in the Middle East. Saudi Arabia, Iraq, and many other Middle Eastern nations were once part of the powerful Ottoman Empire. Iraq was founded after the collapse of this realm at the end of World War I in 1918. British diplomats drew Iraq's new borders, and Britain and France had declared mandates in the Middle East—territories they controlled through local administrators. These mandates included Syria, Lebanon, Jordan, and

Palestine (now Israel). Foreign control of the Middle Eastern states ended after World War II. Kuwait was one of the last; it declared its independence from Britain in 1961. As self-governing nations, the Arab states of the Middle East strongly opposed the presence of foreign military forces—particularly those of the United States and Europe—in the region.

To gain support for military action, the United States reached out to several Arab nations, including Egypt, Morocco, Bahrain, the United Arab Emirates, and Syria. The willingness of these states to join the coalition gave Saudi Arabia some cover for admitting US air and ground forces on its territory. The coalition also gained important allies in Europe, including France, Italy, and Germany. Japan—a nation heavily dependent on Middle Eastern oil—joined the coalition, as did the Soviet Union, a longtime rival of the United States. Great Britain, under the leadership of Prime Minister Margaret Thatcher, also committed immediately to support the coalition. "Oil is vital to the economy of the world," Thatcher later commented in an interview. "If you didn't stop him [Saddam Hussein], and didn't turn him back, he would have gone over the border to Saudi Arabia, over to Bahrain, to Dubai . . . and right down the west side of the Gulf and in fact could have got access and control of 65% of the world's oil reserves, from which he could have blackmailed every nation."[5]

But before putting their troops on the front lines, these states supported economic warfare. On August 6 the UN Security Council passed Resolution 661, placing an international embargo (ban) on trade with Iraq. Nearly every nation in the world agreed not to buy Iraqi goods, including oil, or to sell or ship their products to Iraq. It was hoped that the embargo would so damage the economy of Iraq that the Iraqi people would rebel against their president. Losing support among his own people, Saddam Hussein might withdraw his army from Kuwait or at least negotiate terms with the Kuwaiti rulers.

The Deadline

US leaders pondered how much time to give the embargo before resorting to military force. If they waited too long, support for war among coalition allies would probably decline. Rushing into an invasion was also off the table: the members of the Security Council believed the best course was to delay any assault, by air or on the ground, until it became obvious the embargo would not succeed.

In the meantime, Saddam Hussein used foreigners trapped in Kuwait and Iraq as hostages. Thousands of Americans, Europeans, and nationals of other countries were prevented from leaving. The US and coalition members demanded that Saddam Hussein allow civilians to

15

travel freely out of Iraq. He replied by announcing that Iraq would treat foreigners as its guests. The Iraqi government rounded up all foreigners and placed them in hotels, where they were guarded around the clock.

The embargo did not convince Saddam Hussein to retreat from Kuwait or to ask for peace terms. Nor did the Iraqi leader respond to the demands for the release of the hostages. Although President Bush and his advisers were in favor of giving the embargo time, the confrontation dragged on for months with no resolution. Convinced that military force would be necessary, the US administration again turned to the UN, requesting that the Security Council set a deadline.

This passed as Resolution 678 on November 29, 1990. Iraq had until January 15, 1991. After that date, if Kuwait was still occupied, the resolution authorized the coalition to use any means necessary to drive the Iraqi army out of Kuwait.

Defying the United Nations

Saddam Hussein was unpersuaded by UN resolutions. In his view, withdrawing his army from Kuwait would represent a humiliating defeat for Iraq. He also believed the Iraqi army, although heavily outnumbered, could defeat the United States and its allies. In his view, it was simply a matter of will. During the 1980s Iraq had fought an eight-year war with Iran, losing over a million troops before the two countries agreed to a cease-fire in 1988. On the other hand, America's last full-scale military conflict, in Vietnam, had ended in a negotiated withdrawal of US forces in 1974.

The Vietnam War had inspired widespread protest in the United States, where media coverage raised anger at what appeared to be a pointless loss of life in a poorly defined cause. "Yours is a society that cannot accept 10,000 dead in one battle,"[6] Saddam Hussein told US diplomat April Glaspie just before invading Kuwait. In the same conversation, Glaspie had commented, "We have no opinion on the Arab-Arab conflicts, like your border disagreement with Kuwait."[7] The Iraqi leader believed this to be a

> "We have no opinion on the Arab-Arab conflicts, like your border disagreement with Kuwait."[7]
>
> —April Glaspie, US ambassador to Iraq

Live from the Gulf War

As US warplanes reached the outskirts of Iraq on the first day of bombing, the Cable News Network (CNN) was ready. With correspondents and cameras stationed in a Baghdad hotel, CNN began history's first live video coverage of a military conflict.

Fascinated by the sights and sounds, viewers in the United States and around the world, including Saddam Hussein, tuned in to watch. CNN reported from US military bases, from Iraqi cities, and from the desert battlefields, and it featured replays of precision-guided bombs hitting targets around Iraq. Viewers saw little of the chaos, death, and suffering on the ground. The effect was to sustain public support for the war. In contrast, the filmed reporting of the fighting during the Vietnam War—which was delivered not live but during the daily televised evening news—soured public opinion against that conflict.

The coverage from the Persian Gulf could be deceptive. CNN also reported in detail on the Patriot missile defense systems the United States had supplied to Saudi Arabia and Israel to combat Iraq's Scud attacks. The Patriot was a ground-to-air system designed to destroy an enemy missile while still in the air. But the Patriot missiles were inaccurate, and few of them came close to the incoming Scuds. One study found that Scud missiles actually did more damage in Israel *after* the Patriot system was deployed. Nevertheless, on television the deployment appeared as a great success. The coverage boosted both CNN's ratings and the fortunes of the Raytheon company, makers of the Patriot.

sign that the United States would not get involved if Iraq invaded its neighbor.

Even if Iraq's decision to invade Kuwait led to war with the United States, Iraq's president was confident that his air defense system, his air force, and his powerful arsenal of missiles would put up an effective fight. Iraq had twenty-four heavily fortified air defense bases operational, with seven thousand surface-to-air missiles and six thousand antiaircraft guns. Iraqi fighter aircraft were protected in hardened shelters and saved for a future planned attack on Saudi Arabia and Israel. With the use of Scud long-range missiles, Saddam Hussein planned to inflict mass civilian casualties in these countries and force the coalition to negotiate for peace.

The Iraqi leader also counted on dissension among the coalition nations to head off any invasion. Several important US allies, including France, opposed direct military action, believing the embargo would eventually succeed. The Soviet Union favored negotiating with Iraq, and several Arab coalition allies were openly reluctant to assist in another Western conquest of an Arab country.

Operation Desert Storm

The January 15 deadline set by the UN came and went. Iraq had not budged from Kuwait or shown any interest in negotiating a withdrawal. On January 17, Operation Desert Storm began. This was the code

US president George H.W. Bush discusses the situation in Kuwait during a news conference at the White House on January 12, 1991, shortly after Congress authorized the use of force to liberate Kuwait.

name for a military attack on Iraq by the United States and its allies. Waves of bombers flew across the Iraq–Saudi Arabia border, attacking Iraq's air defense systems. F-117 stealth fighters, designed to escape detection by antiaircraft systems, targeted Iraqi radar stations and a central command base. Over a few days, the assault destroyed Iraq's antiaircraft network.

The allied campaign then turned its attention to military bases, government buildings, factories, airfields, communications systems, oil refineries, and roads. British JP-233 aircraft flew low over Iraqi air bases, dropping clusters of small bombs to blow craters in runways. Tomahawk cruise missiles fired from US ships in the Persian Gulf blasted military installations in Iraqi cities. The missiles had a range of 1,500 miles (2,414 km) and relied on an onboard terrain-mapping computer to follow main streets and turn corners to find their targets. Other smart bombs dropped from the sky carried small video cameras. Using video feeds and laser guidance systems, pilots targeted tanks, artillery pieces, infantry units, and military bases in and around Kuwait City.

The campaign also placed a high priority on Iraq's unconventional arsenal, including chemical and biological weapons and nuclear weapons facilities. The attacks did not completely wipe out Iraq's nuclear facilities, however. Scientists who later escaped Iraq claimed that the country managed to save its nuclear weapons program and a store of chemical weapons.

The Scud Counterattack

With its air force and air-control systems heavily damaged, Iraq could not contest the skies. Iraqi warplanes that did make it into the air were quickly shot down. Most antiaircraft guns were put out of commission on the first day of bombing.

But Iraq had protected its Scud cruise missiles. These liquid-fueled rockets, imported from the Soviet Union, could be launched from fixed or mobile platforms and could carry 2,000-pound (907-kg) explosive warheads or chemical or biological weapons. From western Iraq, they could reach the major cities of Israel. The Jewish state was still at odds with many Arab countries in the Middle East, including Syria and Iran. If Israel could be drawn into a war with Iraq, Saddam Hussein believed these states would drop out of the coalition and join him as allies.

Armed with missiles, US Air Force and Royal Saudi Air Force fighter aircraft conduct a mission during Operation Desert Storm, the military attack on Iraq's air force and air-control systems.

Soon after the air campaign began, he ordered Scuds launched against Israel and US military installations in Saudi Arabia. His goal was to create mass casualties among the Americans and goad the Israelis into a counterattack, possibly an air raid on Baghdad. A total of forty missiles landed on Israel and forty-six on Saudi Arabia. The Scuds did little damage, however. They were difficult to aim or control and flew erratically. Although a few Israeli citizens died in the Scud attacks, the Israeli government did not retaliate.

The Ground War

Operation Desert Storm failed to dislodge the Iraqi army from Kuwait. On January 20, 1991, Saddam Hussein declared, "When the battle becomes a comprehensive one with all types of weapons, the deaths on the allied side will be increased with God's help. When the deaths and dead mount on them, the infidels will leave and the flag of Allahu Akbar [Arabic for God Is Greater] will fly over the mother of all battles."[8] With the Iraqi nation behind him, the coalition bickering over war aims, and President Bush losing support at home, Saddam Hussein was convinced the conflict would break decisively in Iraq's favor.

The ground phase of the war, code-named Operation Desert Sabre, began on February 24. The US Army and Marines, as well as British and French infantry and armored units, stormed across the Iraq border and into Kuwait. Temporary air bases were set up on Iraqi territory to allow helicopters to join the attack. Tanks, armored cars, and artillery quickly overwhelmed Iraqi defenders, most of whom had dug simple trenches to fortify their positions in the flat and stony desert. Two US Marine divisions crossing into Kuwait faced minefields, entrenched troops, barbed wire, and scattered tank and artillery defenses. After putting up a token resistance, however, most Iraqi defenders surrendered, leaving a clear path for US troops to Kuwait City. A second phase of the ground war targeted the elite Republican Guard units in southern Iraq—with similar success. Formed to protect the Iraqi regime from its internal enemies, the Republican Guard was better equipped and better trained than the conventional armed forces, and guard units were the first to enter Kuwait during the initial invasion. On February 28, 1991, after just four days of fighting, President Bush declared a cease-fire that brought an end to the ground war.

Bush had decided not to pursue Iraq's army back to the capital. An assault on Baghdad would mean difficult street fighting, causing heavy casualties among both coalition soldiers and civilians. In addition, the UN resolutions that authorized the use of force did not call for the occupation of Iraq or the overthrow of the country's leader. Many of the coalition allies did not support a full-scale invasion of Iraq; in their view, the goal of the war—the liberation of Kuwait—had already been accomplished.

Kurdish and Shiite Uprisings

President Bush made no secret of his desire to see Saddam Hussein overthrown—or dead. In a radio broadcast of March 1, Bush declared, "In my own view, the Iraqi people should put [Saddam Hussein] aside, and that would facilitate the resolution of all these problems that exist and certainly would facilitate the acceptance of Iraq back into the family of peace-loving nations."[9]

With these words, Bush encouraged Saddam Hussein's enemies inside Iraq to rise up against their leader. The Kurds of northern Iraq were an ethnic minority who opposed the rule of Saddam Hussein. Shiites, concentrated in the south, made up one of the two principal sects of Islam, and one largely deprived of any political power in the Iraqi leader's Sunni-dominated government. The uprisings began in early March 1991 and continued for several weeks. Despite Bush's encouragement to the rebels, US forces offered no real support; their focus remained on change to protecting the remaining coalition troops. Using helicopter gunships and chemical weapons, Iraq's elite Republican Guard units carried out a brutal repression of the Kurds and the Shiites. Thousands of rebel fighters and civilians died in the failed uprising.

By the end of the war, the Iraqi army had lost about 3,700 tanks, 1,856 armored personnel carriers, and 2,140 artillery pieces. Estimates by Iraq of the country's own casualties were 20,000 dead, including 1,000 civilians, and 60,000 wounded. Casualties among the coalition forces were 240 dead and 776 wounded in action.

> "O Iraqis, you triumphed when you stood with all this vigour against the armies of thirty countries. You have succeeded in demolishing the aura of the United States, the empire of evil, terror, and aggression."[10]
>
> —Saddam Hussein

The Persian Gulf War was a victory for the United States and its coalition allies, but Saddam Hussein had survived and, on the day of the cease-fire, struck a defiant pose:

O Iraqis, you triumphed when you stood with all this vigour against the armies of thirty countries. You have succeeded in demolishing the aura of the United States, the empire of evil, terror, and aggression. . . . We are confident that President Bush would have never accepted a cease-fire had he not been informed by his military leaders of the need to preserve the forces fleeing the fist of the heroic men of the Republican Guard.[10]

Coalition Partners

One of the lessons of World War II and the Vietnam War was the importance of establishing a coalition of nations fighting together rather than one nation going it alone. During World War II, more than fifty nations joined together to take on—and defeat—Nazi Germany and its ally Japan. During the Vietnam War, the United States fought largely alone, with help from guerrilla units raised in Vietnam and Laos. This strategy ended in defeat. After Iraq invaded Kuwait, the United States enlisted dozens of countries to help liberate Kuwait and worked to pass resolutions in the UN Security Council.

By the start of the air war in January 1991, twenty-eight countries had contributed 670,000 troops; the coalition included 425,000 troops from the United States. Financial help was also sought, and in this effort the US government sought money from Kuwait, Saudi Arabia, and other Middle Eastern nations. Out of a total cost of $61 billion, a total of $36 billion was contributed by Arab countries, and $16 billion came from Germany and Japan.

The fighting had liberated Kuwait, preserved the borders of Saudi Arabia, and dealt a blow to the Iraqi regime. Even so, the United States would spend the next decade trying, and failing, to subdue Iraq and force Saddam Hussein from power. The many issues between the two countries—economic sanctions, no-fly zones, and the use of unconventional weapons stockpiled by Iraq—would bring about another war in the Persian Gulf just twelve years later.

CHAPTER TWO

How Did Oil Politics Fuel the Gulf War?

Focus Questions

1. How could the Organization of Petroleum Exporting Countries have responded differently to Iraq's concerns about Kuwait, and would a different response have avoided war? Why or why not?
2. How could the United States have responded differently to Iraq's concerns about Kuwait, and would a different response have avoided war? Why or why not?
3. Do you believe concerns about oil prices and supply and their effect on the global economy are legitimate reasons to go to war? Why or why not?

Iraq and Kuwait are both important oil producers and members of the Organization of Petroleum Exporting Countries (OPEC). This group, which also includes Saudi Arabia and other Middle Eastern states, had imposed a global oil embargo in 1973 to protest US assistance to Israel during the Yom Kippur War between Israel and the Arab states of Egypt and Syria. The embargo caused oil shortages worldwide and a spike in energy costs. Although OPEC eventually lifted the embargo, the Arab-Israeli conflicts continued. The US government grew concerned over the supply of Middle Eastern oil, and in 1980 President Jimmy Carter declared, "An attempt by any outside force to gain control of the Persian Gulf region will be regarded as an assault on the vital interests of the United States of America. Such an assault will be repelled by any means necessary, including military force."[11]

In the years before the Persian Gulf War, OPEC's members were frequently at odds over production targets set by the group at its regular meetings. Following the law of supply and demand, when OPEC increased oil production targets, market prices tended to fall; when it decreased those targets, prices usually rose. At OPEC meetings, Iraq demanded production cuts to increase its oil revenues. This would help the country pay some of the massive debts it had incurred to Kuwait and other countries during the Iran-Iraq War of 1980 through 1988. Kuwait and other wealthy producers opposed production cuts, however. They sought to keep the prices level and the demand high among their customers.

Iraq's oil industry faced a range of other problems. The war with Iran had extensively damaged its oil production facilities. Much of its equipment was in poor repair or outdated. Iraq had also nationalized its oil industry during the 1960s, prohibiting foreign ownership of its oil resources. As a result, foreign investment in the Iraqi oil industry dropped, while Kuwait and Saudi Arabia became oil-exporting superpowers. One of the toughest problems Iraq faced, however, was neither political nor economic. It was, instead, a simple matter of geography.

> "An attempt by any outside force to gain control of the Persian Gulf region will be regarded as an assault on the vital interests of the United States of America."[11]
>
> —President Jimmy Carter

OPEC Rivalries

Iraq's geography makes exporting its oil a challenge. The country has limited access to the Persian Gulf, through which most Middle Eastern oil tankers must travel. Just two narrow waterways in southern Iraq allow access for oceangoing oil tankers. These channels were, and still are, Iraq's economic lifeline. One of them runs for part of its length through Kuwaiti waters. In addition, the main Iraqi port at Umm Qasr—where the water is too shallow to handle big tankers—had been severely damaged during the war with Iran.

Iraq earned more than half of its trade income from oil. Any interruption in exports, or any fall in the price of oil, would do serious harm to the Iraqi economy. If exports through the Persian Gulf were stopped, only tanker trucks and oil pipelines stretching across western Iraq were available to ship Iraqi oil abroad. These were much more costly and unreliable methods of getting oil to the international market.

A portrait of Iraqi president Saddam Hussein marks the entrance of an oil refinery in Iraq. Damage to refineries from the Iran-Iraq War, in addition to outdated equipment, nearly decimated Iraq's oil production.

For the Kuwaitis, the oil business was even more important. The country is small, with only one major city and very little manufacturing. But Kuwait had become one of the world's wealthiest nations by relying on oil for 95 percent of its export revenues. Kuwaiti citizens enjoyed a higher standard of living than most Iraqis. To maintain this position, Kuwait's rulers had remained neutral, and uninvolved, during Iraq's long war with Iran. However, Kuwait did extend $14 billion in loans to support the Iraq war effort—and it expected these loans to be paid back, in full.

With the Iran-Iraq War ending in 1988, Kuwait's oil policy now directly clashed with that of Iraq. Instead of cutting production, Kuwait sought to keep its output steady or allow it to rise. By keeping prices stable, the Kuwaiti oil industry benefited from steady demand (oil consumers tend to cut their use of energy, or turn to less expensive substitutes for oil, when prices rise). At OPEC meetings, the Kuwaitis usually opposed actions that would raise market prices.

In any case, compliance with OPEC's production quotas was voluntary. There was no way for the organization to enforce its production targets. It was common for OPEC members to ignore these targets altogether. Iraq could not force Kuwait to cut production, outside of the threats that grew more menacing through the summer of 1990. Behind this controversy lay another issue: Iraq's claim that Kuwait had been stealing oil from Iraqi territory.

Accusations of Oil Theft

Iraq's Rumaili oil field lies in the southeastern part of the country, adjacent to its border with Kuwait. Before the invasion of Kuwait, 225 separate oil wells operated in the region. During the Iran-Iraq War, the Iraqi military had placed explosive mines throughout the Rumaili oil field, making it difficult to continue drilling and operating the wells. Kuwait, seeing an opportunity, began a side-drilling operation in which oil was pumped horizontally from underneath Iraqi territory.

Many oil fields run across national boundaries, and it is common for nations to strike agreements to share oil resources. Iraq had always refused to make such a deal with Kuwait. Now the Iraqis accused Kuwait of stealing Iraqi oil and deliberately undermining the Iraqi economy. But instead of negotiating, Iraq demanded that Kuwait pay $2.4 billion for the oil it had drawn from the Rumaili oil field. In addition, it insisted that side drilling must cease and Kuwait must lease two of its Persian Gulf islands (Bubiyan and Warbah) to Iraq for use as oil-transport stations. Kuwait responded to Iraq's complaints by increasing oil production and refusing to lease any of its territory. Kuwait's rulers believed that doing so would only lead to more Iraqi demands for Kuwaiti land.

The oil dispute between Iraq and Kuwait grew heated in the spring of 1990. To solve the issue, a diplomatic group known as the Arab

League called an emergency meeting in May. At the meeting, Saddam Hussein claimed that the theft of his country's oil, and the drop in oil prices, was costing Iraq $14 billion a year. "We cannot tolerate this kind of economic warfare," Saddam Hussein remarked. "We have reached a state of affairs where we cannot take the pressure."[12]

Taking wary note of the dispute was Saudi Arabia. The main Saudi oil fields lay in the eastern and northeastern parts of the country, not far from the Persian Gulf and Iraq. Saddam Hussein was not friendly with Saudi Arabia, whose rulers he considered rivals for political leadership in the Arab world. With a much smaller military than Iraq, the Saudi rulers knew they would face a dire situation if the Iraqi leader ordered his army to cross the Saudi border. Watching these many conflicts with a worried eye were the oil-importing nations all over the globe that depended heavily on oil from the Middle East.

After amassing substantial war debt and accusing Kuwait of stealing oil from Iraqi territory, Saddam Hussein (pictured in a trench alongside soldiers during the Iran-Iraq War) believed his regime was threatened and ordered an invasion of Kuwait.

The View from Abroad

During the 1980s oil exports through the Persian Gulf accounted for more than half of the world's oil consumption. European countries were more dependent on Middle Eastern oil than the United States, and Japan—with no oil resources of its own—was entirely dependent on imported oil. Any interruption in the supply of oil would send a shock wave through the global economy.

Oil was plentiful in early 1990. The market price declined to eighteen dollars a barrel, with both Kuwait and Iraq producing above their OPEC quotas. Saddam Hussein believed that oil importers were willing and able to pay more—as much as twenty-five dollars a barrel—before they would make any serious effort to cut consumption. In addition to demanding production cuts, he called on Kuwait to contribute $10 billion to Iraq's rebuilding efforts in the aftermath of the Iran-Iraq War and to compensate Iraq for oil he contended had been stolen from the Rumaili oil field. Kuwait's rulers flatly refused these demands. However, they did offer $500 million to assist in the reconstruction of Iraq. In exchange, Kuwait demanded that Iraq resolve its claim on the Warbah and Bubiyan islands and all other boundary disputes.

In the summer of 1990, Kuwait bowed to pressure from Saudi Arabia and Iran—both of which also supported production cuts— to meet some of Saddam Hussein's demands. Most importantly, the Kuwaitis agreed to abide by OPEC production quotas but would not forgive Iraq's war debts. Instead of accepting this concession, Iraq's leader issued more threats and backed them up by moving his military forces close to the Kuwaiti border, an action that seriously alarmed the US government.

Alarm in Washington

The United States had been closely involved with Middle Eastern affairs since the end of World War II in 1945. The American government formed close ties with Saudi Arabia and with Israel. And when war broke out between Iraq and Iran, the US government had sided with Iraq, mainly to keep oil flowing freely from Saudi Arabia and other Persian Gulf producers.

With the oil price in decline, at first there seemed no reason to intervene in the Iraq-Kuwait dispute. Nor was the Bush administration concerned by the increase in oil prices that might come with better cooperation among the OPEC nations. A firm price of twenty-five to thirty dollars per barrel would do little harm to the American economy; instead, it would actually help US oil producers improve their own profit margins and stay competitive with foreign producers.

Threats against Saudi Arabia were a different story. The Iraqi army would have little trouble capturing Saudi oil fields if Saddam Hussein ordered an invasion. This would mean a price spike that would harm the US economy. In an attempt to head off this scenario, the United States persuaded Hosni Mubarak, the president of Egypt, to meet with his Iraqi counterpart to gauge Iraq's intentions. At the meeting, which took place on July 24, 1990, Saddam Hussein admitted that he would still be willing to accept concessions from Kuwait on oil production quotas and on Iraq's war debt. The military maneuvers were still just a way to threaten Kuwait. Saddam Hussein asked Mubarak not to reveal that fact to the Kuwaiti rulers.

The meeting angered Mubarak, who believed Saddam Hussein was trying to manipulate him. He traveled to Kuwait and explained to the Kuwaiti rulers that Iraq would probably accept an offer of money to stand its military down. This convinced the Kuwaitis that the Iraqi leader was bluffing and had no intention of invading.

> "We too can harm you. Everyone can cause harm according to their ability and their size. We cannot come all the way to you in the United States, but individual Arabs may reach you."[13]
>
> —Saddam Hussein

In his speeches and writings, Saddam Hussein declared that Iraq was now in an economic war. This was not only harming the Iraqis, he felt, but also threatening him personally. Having just been through eight years of war, the Iraqi people would see him as a failure, unable to stand up to his much weaker rivals in tiny Kuwait. He believed his regime, and his life, would be under a serious threat, and the only way to prevent this scenario would be to make threats of his own.

In a comment released after Saddam Hussein's fateful meeting with US ambassador April Glaspie, the Iraqi leader sent a blunt mes-

A Sea of Oil

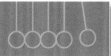

The central cause of the Persian Gulf War was an accident of geography and geology. A virtual ocean of easily accessible oil, by far the largest reserve in the world, lies beneath the countries along the Persian Gulf. Despite decades of extraction, in the years before the war reserves of recoverable oil in the region actually increased. A total of 398 billion barrels of such reserves had been identified there in 1985; just three years later that total reached 572 billion barrels. In an attempt to reduce the dependence on this resource, oil companies carried out extensive, and expensive, oil exploration in non-Gulf regions. But the total proven reserves outside of the Persian Gulf remained steady, neither increasing nor decreasing. Thus the Persian Gulf region maintained its status as one of the world's most productive and important sources of oil.

sage to the Bush administration: "If you use pressure, we will deploy pressure and force. We know that you can harm us although we do not threaten you. But we too can harm you. Everyone can cause harm according to their ability and their size. We cannot come all the way to you in the United States, but individual Arabs may reach you."[13]

The Response to Invasion

Up to this point, President Bush and his advisers had considered the Iraqi leader's comments to be mostly bluster aimed at propping up Saddam Hussein's image as a defender of the Arabs against the West. Their view changed after Iraq made good on its threats and invaded Kuwait. American leaders feared that if the Iraqi army continued into the Saudi oil fields, Iraq would be able to slow or halt the flow of oil from the Middle East, control market prices, and deal serious damage to the global economy.

But the economic motive for war, in the view of the president and his advisers, would not play well with the public. Instead, opposition to the war would remain strong in Congress and among American voters, and the US government would have a hard time enlisting allies. In an interview with *Time* magazine, a US official succinctly explained the issue: "Even a dolt understands the principle. We need the oil. It's nice to talk about standing up for freedom, but Kuwait and Saudi Arabia are not exactly democracies, and if their principal export were oranges, a mid-level State Department official would have issued a statement and we would have closed Washington down for August."[14]

That threat was seen as justification for a military response. President Bush and his advisers, however, denied that access to oil was their first consideration. Instead, in his speeches and press conferences, Bush claimed that Iraq had violated international norms of behavior. If allowed to stand, Bush warned, the Iraqi invasion would embolden dictators around the world. The United States was prepared to fight for freedom and liberty, wherever it was under threat. In an interview conducted by the documentary series *Frontline* after the war, US secretary of state Colin Powell was asked if Kuwait was worth fighting a war over. His reply laid out the official Bush administration view: "I think that was the question. Did [Kuwait] measure up as a regime, as a na-

A Saudi official stands on a pier by an oil facility. During the Iraqi invasion of Kuwait, Saudi Arabia boosted its own oil production, creating an economic boon for multinational oil companies.

The Environmental Aftermath

The ground war that began in January 1991 caused a chaotic retreat by Iraqi units from Kuwait. On orders from Saddam Hussein, these forces attempted to destroy Kuwait's oil infrastructure. High explosives were placed in more than seven hundred oil wells, refineries, tank farms, and other structures. The massive fires gave rise to smoke plumes stretching more than 100 miles (161 km) to the south and southeast over the Persian Gulf. Skies throughout the region were darkened with smoke and oil residue.

While still in Kuwait, the Iraqis also built long oil trenches and then set them afire to interfere with the movement of coalition forces on the ground. These efforts followed a deliberate oil spill engineered along Kuwait's coast, carried out to interfere with any amphibious landing planned by the US Marines. At one point, the spill stretched over 100 miles (161 km) long and 40 miles (64 km) wide.

The fires continued for two months, during which time up to 6 million barrels of oil burned off every day. Military demining units had to thoroughly search for and defuse Iraqi mines in the vicinity of the wellheads before civilian crews could get to work. The first well was capped in April 1991, and it took several more months to finish the job. Kuwait also spent years repairing the damage to refineries, ports, and other oil industry infrastructure.

tion and, frankly, as the source of twenty percent of the world's oil. So it seemed to me that Kuwait did measure up, it was worth an effort to get the Iraqi army out of Kuwait and restore it to its legitimate status."[15]

Oil Markets Survive

The invasion of Kuwait by Iraq on August 2, 1990, did not drive oil prices higher, as widely feared. Saudi Arabia boosted its own production to compensate for the loss of Iraqi oil. In fact, late 1990 and early 1991—while Iraq occupied Kuwait—were boom times for multinational oil companies. While wholesale prices declined somewhat, retail prices jumped, allowing these businesses much larger profit margins. One executive of British Petroleum declared that an increase of one dollar in the wholesale market price of oil meant a $200 million jump in net income for his company.

The start of the ground war in January saw the biggest one-day decrease in oil prices in history—more than ten dollars a barrel. Commodity markets move according to expectations, not necessarily daily or current events. Oil traders believed that the ground war would mean a quick victory for the coalition forces, which in turn meant a glut of oil from liberated Kuwait and an Iraqi oil industry that would eventually be free of embargo.

International oil markets stabilized after the war, despite the interruption in supply. OPEC continued to debate production targets, with limited ability to enforce these targets among its members. Oil politics continued to play a crucial role in the Middle East. Saddam Hussein and his regime survived the war, but the United States stood ready to reimpose the embargo on the country's foreign trade. Protecting its supply of oil remained a key strategic interest for the United States—worth the risk of American lives, if necessary.

CHAPTER THREE

How Did the Cold War's End Influence the Persian Gulf Conflict?

Focus Questions

1. Why did the Soviet Union refuse to support Iraq during the Persian Gulf War, and how did this decision influence the course of events?
2. Why did Arab states such as Egypt and Syria doubt Saddam Hussein's claim that he was fighting for the Arab cause?
3. How could Mikhail Gorbachev have more effectively tried to prevent the Persian Gulf War, and would these efforts have altered the outcome?

The end of World War II in 1945 changed the political map of Europe. Eastern European governments allied themselves with the Soviet Union. Western Europe sided with the United States. The Cold War between the two superpowers followed; it intensified through the 1950s and lasted well into the 1980s. The Soviet-backed government in East Germany built the Berlin Wall to prevent citizens from escaping to the West. The Berlin Wall became a powerful symbol of the high barriers between two very different political systems.

Unlike a so-called hot war—an all-out military confrontation—the Cold War was characterized by both nations probing and prodding for weak points to exploit. In this effort, they sought allies to strengthen their positions as world powers. In the Middle East, Iraq, Egypt, and Syria drew closer to the Soviet Union, and Israel and Saudi Arabia allied with the United States.

Proxy wars were another feature of the Cold War. Over a period of four decades, the United States and Soviet Union involved themselves in numerous conflicts between client states (nations that were politically, militarily, or economically dependent on the larger powers). The super-powers deployed their military advisers, money, weapons, and sometimes troops. Neither the Americans nor the Soviets—both of whom possessed nuclear weapons—sought direct confrontation in these conflicts. Rather, their goal was to exert influence. In the Middle East, for instance, the United States backed Israel in its conflicts with neighboring Arab countries, and the Soviet government supported pan-Arab nationalist movements. Pan-Arab nationalism promoted the ideal of cultural and political unity among Arab countries. This ideal found strong support in Syria, Egypt, and Iraq. After pan-Arab military leaders seized the Iraqi government in 1958, the Soviet Union became a major supplier of weapons to Iraq.

Yet another proxy war between the Soviets and Americans began in December 1979, when the Soviet Union invaded Afghanistan. The Soviets placed a friendly government in charge in Kabul, the Afghan capital. The United States backed Afghan guerrilla fighters, or mujahideen, who opposed the Soviet presence in their country. The mountainous terrain and skilled opposition fighters bogged the Soviet army down in a long, bloody, and fruitless occupation.

Détente

In 1985, in the midst of the Afghan conflict, Soviet president Mikhail Gorbachev concluded that the war was needlessly draining resources from a weakened Soviet economy. With little foreign trade and a declining manufacturing sector, the Soviet Union was hard-pressed to provide even basic consumer goods and food to its people. Realizing that economic reforms were needed, Gorbachev began an effort to end the Cold War and develop some diplomatic cooperation with Western Europe and the United States.

The Soviet Union withdrew its last troops from Afghanistan in early 1989. This began a chain of events that changed the political map of Europe and brought about the fall of the Soviet Union. The Berlin Wall came down, and Eastern European nations opened their borders and overthrew their Soviet-allied governments. Former Soviet-controlled countries such as Poland, Hungary, and Czechoslovakia held elections and adopted new multiparty systems.

Soviet Union troops begin withdrawing from Afghanistan in 1988 after years of battling US-backed mujahideen fighters. The withdrawal helped ease Cold War tensions and develop diplomatic cooperation between the Soviet Union and the United States and its allies.

The Iraq invasion of Kuwait in 1990 provided Gorbachev with further opportunities for détente—a relaxing of tensions with the West. His ultimate goal was to improve trade, domestic economic activity, and living standards for Soviet citizens. As part of this effort, the Soviet president showed a willingness to cooperate with the UN Security Council, whose permanent members included the United States, France, the United Kingdom, the People's Republic of China, and the Soviet Union. Measures of the Security Council were subject to vetoes ("no" votes) by any of these five nations. This often led to stalemates when the body tried to pass resolutions.

Instead of challenging the US response to the invasion of Kuwait, the Soviet leader condemned Iraq and cooperated with the United States in forging the Security Council resolutions. These resolutions, including the strict trade embargo on Iraq, framed the American response to the invasion. At the same time, the United States called

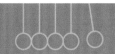

The United States had another important Cold War rival: the People's Republic of China. Although China had broken off its alliance with the Soviet Union, it remained an important force in international affairs, as it held veto power as one of the permanent members of the UN Security Council. The Chinese were going through their own transformation from a rigorous Communist state to one with a hybrid economic system, still under the one-party system devised by China's Communist leader, Mao Tse-tung, after the Chinese revolution. Iraq had been one of China's best customers for arms sales during the 1980s.

Yet in 1989 the Chinese military carried out a massacre of protesters in Tiananmen Square, the main square of the Chinese capital in Beijing. This led to China being roundly shunned by the Western powers, a situation that Chinese leaders wanted to reverse. China cooperated with the United States during the Persian Gulf War by abstaining on any votes in the Security Council—neither voting for nor against. This would at least allow the United States to persuade the other members of the council to support the resolutions.

on its allies, including Arab nations such as Egypt and Morocco, to help present a united international front against Saddam Hussein. Gorbachev became an arbiter in Iraq's dispute with Kuwait and spoke forcefully of the need to resolve the conflict peacefully.

Fighting for the Arab Cause

Saddam Hussein had long considered himself to be a champion of the Arab cause throughout the Middle East. He tried to cast his war with Iran (a Persian, non-Arab nation) as a war fought on behalf of the Arab world. He also characterized his championing of Palestinian Arabs displaced by the founding of Israel in that same light. In addition, the Iraqi leader declared that the arrival of US troops in Saudi Arabia, which began just days after the invasion of Kuwait, meant the return of Western colonialism to the Middle East. The main concern of the United States, Saddam Hussein claimed, was not the freedom of Kuwait but rather control of the only natural resource the Arabs had—oil. The Iraqi leader hoped to exploit the Cold War rivalry of the United States and the Soviet Union as a means of achieving his ultimate goal of annexing Kuwait as an Iraqi province.

His efforts to win broad support among Arab and former Soviet-controlled countries failed. Egypt, Syria, Saudi Arabia, and Morocco all joined the US-led coalition, as did the former Soviet satellites of Poland, Czechoslovakia, and Hungary. In Iraq's war with Kuwait, its only reliable ally was Jordan, a small kingdom on Iraq's western border. The Jordanians had close economic ties with Iraq and provided the Iraqis the only route around the UN trade embargo. During the Persian Gulf War, Jordan's King Hussein (no relation to Saddam Hussein) remarked that "this war is a war against all Arabs and all Muslims and not against Iraq alone."[16]

The final insult came from the Soviet Union, which condemned outright the Iraqi invasion of Kuwait. This stance angered the Iraqi leader, who believed that the Soviets would support him in the attempt to undermine US influence in the Middle East. But Saddam Hussein was playing by an old Cold War script, one that Gorbachev had rewritten. The main concern of Gorbachev and his government in August 1990 was to survive an economic crisis, and to do that, the country needed Western assistance, not a military confrontation.

> "This war is a war against all Arabs and all Muslims and not against Iraq alone."[16]
>
> —King Hussein of Jordan

Diplomatic Maneuvering

In early September 1990 the Soviet Union and the United States agreed to an emergency summit meeting in Helsinki, Finland. This was the first high-level conference designed to resolve Iraq's occupation of Kuwait. The meeting greatly alarmed Saddam Hussein, who immediately asked Gorbachev to meet with Iraq's foreign minister. Hoping to gain assurances of Soviet support, Saddam Hussein instead found that Gorbachev strongly opposed the invasion of Kuwait. Gorbachev took the opportunity to strongly criticize the Iraqi actions: "What you did was an act of aggression and we cannot and will not

Soviet president Mikhail Gorbachev (far right) meets with Iraqi foreign minister Tariq Aziz (at left) and other officials in Moscow in order to persuade Iraq to withdraw from Kuwait and prevent the ground offensive by US and allied forces.

back you in any way," declared Gorbachev. "We are ready to help on the basis of complete withdrawal."[17]

This was not the response Saddam Hussein had expected or hoped for. He countered that his invasion was a restoration of Iraq to its historic borders, and was justified by the hostile actions of the Kuwaiti rulers. He also now characterized the conflict as an internal affair between Arabs, stating that the superpowers should stand back and allow Iraq and Kuwait to settle it themselves. He also declared that Iraqis were again fighting and dying for Arab interests, as they had during the Iran-Iraq War. Rather than making war on Kuwait, he was opposing the hostile invasion of Saudi Arabia by the United States and its allies. To prove his good intentions, he offered to hold a conference to resolve the two major disputes now troubling the region: the situation in Kuwait, as well as the demands of the displaced Palestinians in Israel.

But with the lessening of Cold War tensions, Soviet allies such as Syria no longer felt bound to Soviet interests or the need to steadfastly oppose US goals in the Middle East. Saddam Hussein found himself without support among most of his Arab neighbors, who saw no benefit to themselves in agreeing to the occupation and annexation of Kuwait.

Passing Resolutions in the UN

Although Gorbachev cooperated with the United States in the UN Security Council, he did not want to see direct US military intervention in the Middle East. He believed the trade sanctions, which banned Iraq from selling its oil and other goods, should be given time and would eventually convince Saddam Hussein to negotiate a withdrawal. Although Iraq was trying to evade the embargo by shipping oil through Jordan, the US Navy was effectively blocking these shipments in the Red Sea. Given time, in Gorbachev's opinion, the economic pain would force Saddam Hussein to change course.

Gorbachev also worked throughout the fall of 1990 to head off an invasion of Iraq. The Soviet Union cooperated with US diplomatic efforts in the United Nations and agreed to support a series of Security Council resolutions demanding Iraq's withdrawal from Kuwait. Instead of fighting for advantage against the Americans, the Soviet government was now trying to forge an agreement between the United States and Iraq. Those efforts did not succeed. The Americans demanded an Iraqi withdrawal from Kuwait before discussion of any other issues. Saddam Hussein said he would agree to a withdrawal only if sanctions were lifted, the problem of Iraqi access to the Persian Gulf was solved, and the United States withdrew completely from Saudi Arabia. The two sides were at an impasse.

In November 1990 came the US push for a new UN resolution calling for the use of force should the embargo fail to work. The Soviet government, at first, pushed back on this idea. James Baker, a top American diplomat, flew to Moscow on November 8. The Russian

> "What you did was an act of aggression and we cannot and will not back you in any way."[17]
>
> —Mikhail Gorbachev, president of the Soviet Union

government was now divided between Arabists—who wanted to keep the anti-Western posture in the Middle East—and a faction more supportive of the US position. Baker pointed out that the United States could not stay indefinitely in Saudi Arabia. The coalition forces would have to end the Iraqi occupation or go home. In addition, Saddam Hussein was willing to sacrifice his own people to sanctions rather than face the humiliating prospect of a withdrawal from Kuwait. To help gain Russian cooperation, Baker briefed the Soviet foreign minister on US military plans for the defeat of Iraq. It was the first instance of full military cooperation between the two countries since World War II.

Gorbachev agreed in principle to a resolution authorizing the use of force, but he wanted to hold off in order to give Iraq further time to cooperate. He assured the Americans that he was not opposed to a deadline, but wanted to make sure Iraq was given plenty of time to comply. Although Kuwait and Britain opposed the setting of a deadline, the United States wanted to show a spirit of cooperation with Gorbachev in order not to undermine his position in the Soviet government.

Lobbying by the United States among the members of the Security Council paid off. (Besides its five permanent members, the Security Council includes fifteen rotating members.) Among those on the council at the time, only Yemen and Cuba were not willing to support a "use of force" resolution. Zaire, France, Britain, Ivory Coast, Ethiopia, Colombia, and Malaysia voted in support, giving the United States a majority. The only disagreement with the Soviets was over the timing of the fixed deadline. Gorbachev originally wanted to set a date of January 31. He also wanted the resolution to describe this waiting period as a goodwill gesture, allowing the Iraqis a final chance to cooperate with the UN demands.

The United States simply did not want to wait that long. The presence of American military forces on Saudi soil, considered holy territory for Muslims, was troublesome for the Saudi regime. The longer that five hundred thousand American troops remained in Saudi Arabia, the more pressure there would be for the United States to accept the Kuwaiti invasion and pull its forces out of the Middle East. Eventually, the Security Council accepted a compromise date. The vote on

Resolution 678 was taken in the Security Council on November 29, setting a deadline for withdrawal on January 15, 1991.

Heading Off Invasion

Even with the start of the air war on January 16, Gorbachev continued his efforts to head off a ground invasion. On February 21, Gorbachev invited Tariq Aziz, Iraq's foreign minister, to an emergency conference in Moscow. After the meeting, Gorbachev spoke to President Bush, claiming that the Iraqis were now willing to meet some conditions to head off the invasion. They would agree to leave Kuwait within twenty-one days, although they would not pay reparations to Kuwait, as demanded by the United States. Nor would they discuss another demand of the Americans—a plan to remove weapons of mass destruction from Iraq's arsenal.

The United Nations and the Use of Force

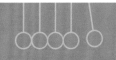

The United Nations provides a place for nations to debate and to resolve their disputes. In theory, the group also allows its members to fight in self-defense. According to Article 51 of the UN Charter, the organization will authorize the use of force if any of its members are attacked. The article says, in part, "Nothing in the present Charter shall impair the inherent right of individual or collective self-defense if an armed attack occurs against a Member of the United Nations, until the Security Council has taken measures necessary to maintain international peace and security."

In the view of the United States, this was not enough to authorize the full-scale invasion of Iraq, which would be the means necessary to eject the Iraqi army from Kuwait. American diplomats proceeded through several months of debate and resolutions before winning a Security Council vote to use any means necessary to defeat the Iraqi occupation.

United Nations, "Charter of the United Nations: Chapter VII," www.un.org/en/sections/un-charter/chapter-vii/.

By this time Saddam Hussein may have realized that the Cold War was no longer a factor in the Middle East. The Soviet Union's interest now lay in cooperative relations with the United States, not with superpower confrontation. That meant, simply, that Iraq could not rely on Soviet support. President Bush also recognized Gorbachev's interest in containing and limiting the conflict. "It is your neighborhood, and some of them are your friends," Bush said to the Soviet leader in a phone call just before the ground attack. "We recognize Soviet interests in the area. I want to get our forces out of there as soon as possible."[18]

Nevertheless, Saddam Hussein continued to defy the United States and the UN resolutions. Instead of starting a withdrawal from Kuwait, he ordered the burning of Kuwait's oil wells to slow down any

A Kuwaiti man watches burning oil fields. In an act of defiance against the United States and UN resolutions, Saddam Hussein ordered the burning of Kuwait's oil wells to slow down the advance of the coalition forces.

advance into Kuwait by the coalition forces. This only prompted the United States to issue another ultimatum on February 22: Iraq must begin a withdrawal from Kuwait within twenty-four hours, before noon on February 23. Just before the deadline, Bush and Gorbachev spoke once again by telephone. Gorbachev argued for giving Iraq more time, but Bush refused. Any move by the Iraqis out of Kuwait would have to take place immediately, he said. Otherwise the ground attack was going ahead.

"We recognize Soviet interests in the area. I want to get our forces out of there as soon as possible."[18]

—President George H.W. Bush

The new era in US-Soviet diplomacy resulted in greater cooperation from the Soviet government with American efforts to reverse Iraq's invasion of Kuwait. At the same time, the détente between the superpowers robbed Saddam Hussein of a vital weapon in his efforts to divide the opposing Cold War factions and to play the Soviet Union and its allies against the United States and its allies. This was key to assembling an international coalition to oppose Iraq, as well as successfully pursuing UN resolutions to sanction the use of force against Iraq in January and February of 1991.

CHAPTER FOUR

What Was the Result of Basing US and Coalition Troops in Saudi Arabia?

Defeating Iraq was not a matter of simply invading Kuwait and ejecting Iraqi forces. The United States believed that the Iraqi army—even after it returned to its own country—still posed a threat to Saudi Arabia. In its long-range military planning, the Bush administration sought to contain this threat—permanently. The Americans wanted a total defeat of Iraqi forces. Once this was accomplished, the United States planned to leave a small force of air and naval assets in the region to protect Kuwait and Saudi Arabia from any possible future attacks. The best outcome, in the view of the Bush administration, was for the military defeat to bring a loss of popular support for Saddam Hussein, the downfall of his regime, and the emergence of a more pro-American government in Iraq.

The Buildup in Saudi Arabia

For American military planners, geography posed a problem for achieving the first phase of this plan. With only a narrow coast facing the Persian Gulf, Iraq was not easily accessible from the sea. A network of canals and marshy coastal lowlands in this region prevented a large-scale ground invasion from the sea. Instead, the Americans prepared an assault by infantry and armored units through the desert wastes of southern Iraq. To mount such an invasion, they would have to establish forward bases on Saudi territory.

The presence of Western military forces on Saudi soil, however, was a sensitive matter. The kingdom by tradition banned non-Muslims in certain regions and cities, and it also banned any non-Muslim religious observances anywhere in its territory. But the Americans saw the mission of protecting Saudi territory from Iraq, and defeating the Iraqi occupation of Kuwait, as more important than any religious concerns. Within days of the Iraqi invasion of Kuwait, the American government requested permission from the Saudi king to break with tradition and allow Western troops in Saudi Arabia.

As part of this effort, President Bush promised the Saudi rulers that the military would heed religious sensibilities and withdraw once the mission was completed. On August 6, 1990, King Fahd bin Abdulaziz al Saud formally granted permission for the United States to deploy forces to Saudi territory. The US buildup in Saudi Arabia, known as Operation Desert Shield, began within twenty-four hours and continued for several months.

The first US units to arrive included two F-15 fighter squadrons, an 82nd Airborne Division quick-deployment group known as a ready brigade, and an airborne warning and control (AWAC) system unit. Compared to the enemy forces poised just across the border in Iraq, this was a token force—nothing more than a speed bump should Saddam Hussein decide to invade the Saudi kingdom. Yet the presence of US troops demonstrated a resolve to resist any attempt by Iraq to cross the Saudi border and, in particular, threaten the kingdom's globally important oil fields.

Deployment to the Desert

Posing as the defender of Muslims and Arabs, Saddam Hussein railed against what he characterized as an invasion of Saudi Arabia. Even as

An Egyptian tank crew awaits orders near the border between Saudi Arabia and Kuwait. Egypt's military and other Arab allies provided thirty-two thousand troops to the coalition to oust Iraqi forces from Kuwait.

he did so, US and other allied troops continued arriving in the region. Over the next two months, the XVIII Airborne Corps deployed with 120,000 troops, 700 tanks, 1,400 armored fighting vehicles, and 600 heavy guns. British and French infantry and armored units also deployed to Saudi Arabia, and Egypt and other Arab allies of the coalition provided 32,000 troops and 400 tanks.

In addition to ground troops, the United States had naval assets in the Persian Gulf blockading Iraq and based air assets in Turkey (lying northwest of Iraq), Qatar (on the Persian Gulf coast to the south), and Saudi Arabia. The US Army Central Command set up a headquarters post in Riyadh, the Saudi capital.

In northern Saudi Arabia, newly arrived American troops began patrolling the desert and building defensive outposts. US and coalition forces trained and maneuvered at night to avoid the midafternoon's furnace heat and blazing sun. During the day, dust and sand kicked up by heavy winds still made problems for the troops and for their equipment, which frequently broke down.

Osama bin Laden

To win support for his decision to allow Western troops into Saudi Arabia, King Fahd turned to Sheikh Abdel-Aziz Bin Baz. As the head of the Supreme Council of the Ulema, the country's Islamic authority, Bin Baz was the senior religious leader in the kingdom. Seeking the sanction of the Ulema, King Fadh requested that the sheikh issue a fatwa, or religious decree. Bin Baz agreed, writing that "the Supreme Council . . . supports what was undertaken by the ruler, may God grant him success: the bringing of forces equipped with instruments capable of frightening and terrorizing the one who wanted to commit an aggression against this country."[19]

The fatwa was generally successful in raising support among leading Saudi clerics for the presence of Western troops. Yet the coalition bases remained a contentious issue for religious dissenters within the kingdom. The presence of thousands of Western troops on Saudi territory was too much for Osama bin Laden, the scion of a wealthy Saudi family. In Bin Laden's view, the presence of foreign, Christian troops in Saudi Arabia recalled the invasion of the Middle East by the Christian Crusaders of medieval times. Like Saddam Hussein, Bin Laden also believed the Americans change to did not have the stomach for a long fight. "Look at Vietnam, look at Lebanon," Bin Laden proclaimed. "Whenever soldiers start coming home in body bags, Americans panic and retreat. Such a country needs only to be confronted with two or three sharp blows, then it will flee in panic, as it always has."[20]

> "The Supreme Council . . . supports what was undertaken by the ruler, may God grant him success: the bringing of forces equipped with instruments capable of frightening and terrorizing the one who wanted to commit an aggression against this country."[19]
>
> —Sheikh Abdel-Aziz Bin Baz

Bin Laden traveled to Riyadh to make a personal appeal to Prince Sultan bin Abdulaziz al Saud, who also served as the Saudi minister of defense. With the help of his connections in the construction industry, Bin Laden claimed he could build effective defenses along the Iraqi border. He also claimed to have a brigade of seasoned Afghan fighters at his disposal, which he was willing to deploy to the Iraqi border to deter any threat from Saddam Hussein.

If dedicated mujahideen living in caves and mountain camps could eject the Soviet army from Afghanistan, Bin Laden argued, then they could certainly deter Hussein from carrying out any threat against Saudi Arabia. The king and prince were not convinced, however. In response to Bin Laden's offer, the prince replied, "there are no caves in Kuwait."[21]

Bin Laden was not making an empty boast, however. As a college student during the 1970s, he took up the ideas of Sheikh Abdullah Azzam, an Islamic scholar who favored the creation of a single pan-Islamic state, or caliphate. The means to create this state would be *jihad*, or a holy war. According to Azzam, all Muslims were under a religious obligation to heed the call to jihad in order to halt the spreading and corrupting influence of the Western world, particularly the United States and Europe, on the Arab nations of the Middle East.

In 1979 Bin Laden moved to Peshawar, Pakistan, to establish a base to fight the Soviet occupation of Afghanistan. Working closely with Azzam, he issued a call to Muslims from all over the world to join the mujahideen forces in Afghanistan. The mujahideen proved to be effective fighters, and the murderous guerrilla warfare finally prompted the Soviets to withdraw from Afghanistan in 1989.

While moving between Pakistan and the remote mujahideen camps in Afghanistan, Bin Laden established a new group, naming it change to al Qaeda, or "the Base," after the name of his headquarters in Peshawar. The mission of al Qaeda was to carry out acts of terrorism against the West. He returned to Saudi Arabia in late 1989, after the Soviet withdrawal from Afghanistan. But the Saudi government saw him as a troublemaker and feared that Bin Laden could damage their relations with Western allies, including the United States. In an attempt to prevent Bin Laden from stirring up trouble abroad, the Saudi government revoked his passport.

The Continuing Presence of US Troops

Bin Laden, however, remained loyal to the Saudi king and royal family through the Persian Gulf War. He believed that the Saudi rulers, in a state of panic, had succumbed to pressure from the United States. He fully expected all Western forces to leave when the war ended.

Much to Bin Laden's surprise and outrage, however, the United States kept naval and air assets in the Persian Gulf region after the defeat of Iraq. US Marine Corps troops also stayed on Saudi territory as part of Joint Task Force Southwest Asia. This force relied on Saudi bases to carry out Operation Southern Watch—the effort to maintain a no-fly zone over southern Iraq. About five thousand US combat troops and air crew members remained in Saudi Arabia. The United Kingdom and France also kept air force training personnel in the kingdom. Believing the Saudi rulers had been intimidated by the

Osama bin Laden conducts a broadcast for al Qaeda in 1998. Bin Laden condemned the United States and its allies for invading Islamic holy lands. He soon ordered and masterminded the deadly attacks of September 11, 2001.

United States, Bin Laden now viewed the Saudi royal family as complicit in an outrageous attack on Islam by the West.

During the 1990s Bin Laden delivered a series of petitions to the Saudi regime demanding, among other things, the removal of all foreign troops. In response, the regime canceled government contracts with the Bin Laden companies and stepped up arrests of religious dissidents. These actions did not calm a growing controversy between conservative clergy in Saudi Arabia and the Saudi government. Bin Laden condemned the regime for abandoning true Islam and for making alliances with Western nations. In a letter dated September 19, 1994, Bin Laden laid out his grievances: "The Saudi government has exposed its hostility to Islam by arresting the best of the ulema. The regime also imported Christian women to defend it, thereby placing the army in the highest degree of shame, disgrace, and frustration."[22] This last comment was a reference to the fact that US military forces included both women and men. The presence of Western women holding equal status to their male counterparts was considered sacrilege in some of the most conservative factions of Islam.

The Crisis

Throughout the Islamic world, the Persian Gulf War gained the nickname of al-Azma, meaning "the Crisis." This referred to the commonly held view that the liberation of Kuwait had not been the true purpose of the war. Rather, in this view, the real goal had been the de-

The Hijaz and Saudi Arabia

The classic holy land of Islam is known as the Hijaz. This region of western Saudi Arabia is home to Mecca and Medina, cities important in the early history of the religion and the life of its founder, the prophet Muhammad. Traditionally, all non-Muslims were barred from living in or visiting Mecca, a law that is still enforced at checkpoints in and around the city. Modern Saudi Arabia still enforces a nationwide ban on non-Islamic religious practices, and it has adopted sharia law, derived from the writings of the Koran, the Islamic holy book.

feat of Islam by the West—and, in particular, by the United States. The continuing presence of US troops on Saudi soil led to calls for acts of terrorism against Western targets and civilians—including coalition forces stationed in Saudi Arabia.

The kingdom experienced a political crisis as rival factions among the royal family vied for power. One group, led by Fahd's brother Prince Sultan, was closely allied to the United States. Another faction, led by Prince Abdullah bin Abdulaziz al Saud, the half-brother of the king and head of Saudi Arabia's National Guard, opposed the US presence and fought to consolidate its hold over the country's armed forces. Abdullah coordinated a terrorist campaign with allies in Iran and Syria and Islamic fundamentalists within Saudi Arabia. The goal was to create confusion and fear, thus strengthening Abdullah's hand against his pro-American rivals. In late 1995 a car bomb exploded in Riyadh, killing five Americans at a training facility for the Saudi National Guard. On June 25, 1996, a truck bomb

> "Not long ago, I gave advice to the Americans to withdraw their troops from Saudi Arabia. Now let us give some advice to the governments of Britain and France to take their troops out."[23]
>
> —Osama bin Laden

detonated at a US Air Force compound in Khobar, killing nineteen US service members and injuring four hundred others.

In an interview with the British newspaper the *Independent*, Bin Laden declared that the Khobar attack marked the start of outright war between Muslims and the United States. He called out the Saudi government for attempting to further Westernize Saudi Arabia and turn it into an economic vassal of the United States.

> Not long ago, I gave advice to the Americans to withdraw their troops from Saudi Arabia. Now let us give some advice to the governments of Britain and France to take their troops out—because what happened in Riyadh and Khobar showed that the people who did this have a deep understanding in choosing their targets. They hit their main enemy, which is the Americans. They killed no secondary enemies, nor their brothers in the army or the police of Saudi Arabia.[23]

Bin Laden returned to Afghanistan, where he set up new headquarters under the protection of the Taliban, the country's Muslim fundamentalist government. On August 7, 1998—the eighth anniversary of the arrival of US troops on Saudi territory—car bombs exploded near US embassies in Kenya and Tanzania, killing 224 people, including 12 Americans. The United States accused Bin Laden of ordering the attacks and retaliated by launching cruise missile attacks against Bin Laden's Afghan camps and against a factory in Khartoum, Sudan's capital, which was suspected of making chemical weapons.

In 2001 Bin Laden, along with other leaders of al Qaeda, drew up plans for their most ambitious attack yet. The group enlisted twenty men to hijack commercial flights in the United States, divert the planes to selected targets in New York City and Washington, DC, and use the planes as guided missiles to destroy their targets and kill as many civilians as possible. The attack took place on September 11,

Life in Dhahran

During the Persian Gulf War—between August 7, 1990, and March 26, 1991—7,248 US aircraft landed in Saudi Arabia. Of those, 6,755 landed in the city of Dhahran. The newly arrived US ground troops and officers found themselves living in a new world, one with strange customs and some very strict rules. Saudi Arabia did not (and still does not) permit the sale or consumption of alcohol, public entertainments such as movies or plays, or non-Muslim religious services of any kind. Women are forbidden to go out alone without an accompanying male, and they are strictly banned from driving.

For those who could drive, transport in Saudi Arabia proved as hazardous as the Iraqi army. After the cease-fire took effect, thirty-one US service members were killed in plane crashes and traffic accidents. Nevertheless, the death rate for the military was actually lower in 1991 than in previous years. This was due to the fact that half a million service members in Saudi Arabia were subject to a ban on alcohol—and alcohol-related traffic accidents are the leading cause of death in the peacetime military.

After the September 11 attacks (pictured are the fallen Twin Towers in New York City), US president George W. Bush vowed to bring its perpetrators to justice. This led to US air strikes and ground assaults in Afghanistan in addition to a second invasion of Iraq in 2003.

2001 (9/11). Three of the planes reached their targets, but a fourth crashed in Pennsylvania after a struggle between the hijackers and passengers. The death toll of more than three thousand made the 9/11 attacks the deadliest terrorist attack ever perpetrated against the United States.

The Second Persian Gulf War

President George W. Bush, son of the man who had led the Persian Gulf War coalition in 1990 through 1991, vowed to avenge the 9/11 attack and bring its planners to justice. In October 2001 the United States began Operation Enduring Freedom. This combined air and ground assault targeted al Qaeda enclaves in the cities and mountain valleys of Afghanistan. The United States also declared war on Afghanistan's Taliban government in the fall of 2001 and then prepared for a second invasion of Iraq in March 2003.

Again, the Saudi government agreed to grant access to some of its military facilities, although no Saudi troops fought in the Second Persian Gulf War. The number of US troops stationed in the kingdom increased to ten thousand, and US commanders used the Prince Sultan Air Base near Riyadh as a command post for their air campaign against Iraq. Saudi Arabia granted overflight rights for US planes and missiles and also provided staging areas for US Special Forces operations into southern Iraq.

More sensitive by this time to their image as staunch American allies, the Saudi government played down their cooperation with the US military. The United States, for its part, announced its withdrawal of troops from Saudi Arabia in April 2003. That summer, in a formal ceremony, the United States transferred Prince Sultan Air Base to the Saudi government. Although the US military had effectively withdrawn from Saudi Arabia, the efforts by Islamic fundamentalists against the West continued in the Middle East and also in Europe. The presence of foreigners on Saudi soil had inspired Bin Laden's global terror campaign, but Islamic fundamentalists held many other grievances against the United States.

CHAPTER FIVE

What Resulted from Allowing Saddam Hussein to Remain in Power?

Focus Questions

1. Do you agree with President George H.W. Bush's decision to allow Saddam Hussein to remain in power after his forces were ousted from Kuwait? Why or why not?
2. Should the United States intervene in the affairs of foreign nations to support politicians who are friendly to US interests? Why or why not?
3. How might the course of events in Iraq have unfolded differently after 9/11 if Saddam Hussein had lived and remained in power in Iraq?

The Persian Gulf War ended faster than anyone had expected. From start to finish, it ran a little less than seven months. The ground campaign alone lasted less than a week. By the time the United States declared a cease-fire on February 28, 1991, the Iraqi army had been ejected from Kuwait, and Saddam Hussein's elite Republican Guard and other troops were in a headlong retreat back to Iraq. Coalition leaders now faced a decision: whether to continue their pursuit of those troops into the heart of Iraq—and Saddam Hussein's seat of power—or halt and go home.

Iraqis in Retreat

Just days before the cease-fire was announced, the Republican Guard units were almost encircled near the town of Basra, 20 miles (32 km) north of the Kuwaiti border. That left a single road still open back to the Iraqi capital of Baghdad. Along the Basra road, a convoy of Iraqi armored vehicles and trucks crept north in a huge traffic jam. Although the coalition generals wanted the Iraqis out of Kuwait, they did not yet have the forces in place to cut off this retreat. Saddam Hussein's army had a good chance to escape to the north and fight another day. In the early morning of February 26, General Buster Glosson, commander of the US Fourteenth Air Division, ordered a dozen F-15E fighter jets to scramble from their bases in Saudi Arabia. The jets quickly reached Highway 80 and attacked the Iraqis. Through the dawn hours and into the afternoon, waves of fighters bombed and strafed the convoy, while long-range heavy artillery opened up as well. Some Iraqis fled the scene on foot, but others tried, and failed, to escape in their vehicles.

The result was a chaotic slaughter of an enemy in retreat. Highway 80 turned into a vast cemetery, with hundreds of Iraqi troops trapped and dead in their trucks and on the ground. The Highway of Death, as General Norman Schwarzkopf later called it, stretched for miles, providing a gruesome picture of war's pitiless destruction.

The next day, at a press briefing, Schwarzkopf—the commander of the coalition forces—reported that the coalition had inflicted a total defeat on the main Iraqi army. Coalition forces, however, were still battling two divisions of the Republican Guard, a force that included seven hundred tanks. In answer to a question, Schwarzkopf declared, "We've accomplished our mission, and when the decision-makers come to the decision that there should be a cease-fire, nobody will be happier than me."[24] Kuwait's liberation—the main objective of the war—had been accomplished. But the decision whether or not to stop the ground offensive lay with the president, who serves as commander in chief of the armed forces.

> "We've accomplished our mission, and when the decision-makers come to the decision that there should be a cease-fire, nobody will be happier than me."[24]
>
> —General Norman Schwarzkopf

The Decision to Halt

With the Iraqi army crumbling, President George H.W. Bush and his advisers considered their options. They could secure Kuwait, set up

Kuwaiti citizens and an American soldier celebrate the liberation of Kuwait from Iraqi forces. The war went on for nearly seven months before the United States declared a cease-fire.

defenses to prevent Saddam Hussein from organizing a counterattack, and halt the coalition advance. Or—with command of the skies and nearly five hundred thousand troops, tanks, artillery, and armored vehicles ready and available—they could order an advance on the roads north to the Iraqi capital of Baghdad. A military conquest of the city would offer the chance to capture and overthrow the Iraqi leader. The Americans could install a new government more compliant with their prime objective: safeguarding the uninterrupted flow of energy resources from the Persian Gulf region.

But an advance on Baghdad raised serious tactical problems. If the coalition forces pressed on, they would likely face an insurgency in the areas of central Iraq that were still loyal to their president. Instead of clear, flat desert, they would be fighting in cities, where enemy units could easily conceal themselves among the civilian population. Their route would be blocked by land mines, bridges and airports would be sabotaged, and supply lines back to Saudi Arabia would grow longer and more vulnerable to attack. Civilian casualties would mount, which would undermine public support for the war. As winter turned to spring, Iraq's hot climate would start to work against ground troops. Seasonal dust storms would interfere with operations on the ground and in the air.

Even if successful, installing a client regime conjured the ghost of Western colonialism. A government allied to and dependent on the United States would be seen as a puppet of the West; many would believe its real purpose was to guarantee American control of Iraq's oil. Such a regime would have little or no support among the Iraqis, or other Arab states in the Middle East, and perhaps even from American allies in Europe. At home, the American public was wary of long-term involvement in foreign countries, especially in

Breaking Iraq in Three

The decision to defeat the Iraqi military but allow the survival of Saddam Hussein's regime did nothing to address continuing civil conflict in Iraq among Sunnis, Shiites, and Kurds. This conflict has prompted some to suggest allowing Iraq to split into three new, independent countries. This would result in a Kurdish state in the north, a Sunni remnant of the former Iraq in the center, and a Shiite-dominated government to control the south and Iraq's outlet to the Persian Gulf.

After the overthrow of Saddam Hussein in 2003, the official position of the United States has remained the same: to keep Iraq together as one country and hope that the Iraqi government can tamp down violence enough to make that possible. This stand assumes that, eventually, the warring sides will accept the notion of peacefully compromising to solve Iraq's problems. Thus far the goal of a united and peaceful Iraq has not been achieved.

turbulent regions where US lives would be at constant risk for little apparent gain.

Considering advice from Secretary of State Colin Powell and a briefing on the military situation from General Schwarzkopf, President Bush made the decision to cease hostilities—without any request for a truce or peace terms from Saddam Hussein. Events along the so-called Highway of Death were a crucial factor in this decision. "The Highway of Death was all over television at that point," recalled Powell in a 2015 interview. "The president said, 'Well, if we've accomplished the mission, and I think we have, then what's the point of killing more people?'"[25] Bush wanted to prevent any further slaughters and allow the United States to appear reasonable and merciful to the Iraqis, to coalition allies, and to the rest of the world.

On March 3, Schwarzkopf met with General Sultan al-Jabburi, the Iraqi army's deputy chief of staff, and ten other Iraqi officers. The American general laid down cease-fire terms: the Iraqis must release all coalition prisoners, return any property taken from Kuwait, release Kuwaiti citizens, and assist with the clearing of mines and booby traps. Al-Jabburi agreed, but he also asked permission to use helicopters for transport since the Iraqi air force had been destroyed and the bombed roads were now impassable. Schwarzkopf agreed, not realizing the very serious consequences of this concession in the looming Iraqi civil war.

The Uprising Begins

Saddam Hussein took the cease-fire as an opportunity to declare victory, claiming to have fought the world's most powerful military to a standstill. Not only had Iraq prevented any further advance by the coalition, he declared, but the foreign troops had been ejected from Iraqi soil, representing an important stand by Arabs against the West.

The Iraqi leader tried to rally support among his people by presenting the defeat as a victory. This ploy had little effect, especially on his many opponents within Iraq. In the northern reaches of the country, the Kurdish population had long demanded an independent Kurdish nation. In the south, Shiite-majority cities such as Karbala, Najaf, and Basra were also growing defiant of the regime. Shiites and Sunnis are the two principal and rival sects of Islam, and Iraq's Sunni-dominated government had made enemies in the south. With its military weakened and its government driven out of Kuwait in a humiliating defeat, Iraq was primed for a civil war.

In a Voice of America radio broadcast in February, President Bush had discussed the problem of Saddam Hussein and the future of Iraq. Bush suggested, "There is another way for the bloodshed to stop, and that is for the Iraqi military and the Iraqi people to take matters into their own hands, to force Saddam Hussein the dictator to step aside."[26] Many of his enemies saw this as a promise by the United States to support an uprising.

"There is another way for the bloodshed to stop, and that is for the Iraqi military and the Iraqi people to take matters into their own hands, to force Saddam Hussein the dictator to step aside."[26]

—President George H.W. Bush

On the same day as Schwarzkopf's meeting with al-Jabburi, an Iraqi tank fired a shell through a portrait of Saddam Hussein in the center of Basra. Shiites in southern Iraq and Kurds in the north took this bold act as the signal for a revolution. Civilians, many of them unarmed, took to the streets of Basra, Karbala, and Mosul—the principal city of the Kurdish north—to seize government buildings, raid arms depots, and free political prisoners. Saddam Hussein's government remained in control of Baghdad and the center of the country.

The Rebellion Is Crushed

At first, the rebellion succeeded. The Iraqi army lost control of fourteen of Iraq's eighteen provinces, while rebel forces marched within a few miles of Baghdad. But powerful Republican Guard units had escaped the war intact, and by the terms laid down by General Schwarzkopf, they still had the use of helicopter gunships. The Republican Guard used these helicopters to seek out and destroy rebel groups in northern and southern Iraq.

Expecting help from the coalition forces still stationed in Saudi Arabia, the rebels soon discovered they were on their own. Even when capable of preventing the Republican Guard assaults, US units in view of the conflict were ordered to stand down. Rebels captured by units

Kurdish civilians seek refuge after fleeing the fighting between the Republican Guard and Kurdish rebels. Saddam Hussein's military unit crushed the Kurdish uprising.

loyal to Saddam Hussein were subject to mass executions; poison gas attacks were carried out on the civilian population. By April 1991 the rebels were in retreat, and refugees were streaming out of the cities in rebel-held areas. Seeking shelter, Kurdish civilians took to the remote mountains along the border of Iraq and Turkey, where thousands died of exposure and starvation. The Iraqi air forces had laid waste to the Shiite holy cities of Najaf and Karbala, where Saddam Hussein ordered the destruction of Shiite mosques and shrines.

Bush and his advisers did not want to involve the US military in a civil war. Nor did they want to lose the solid international support that had made the operation to free Kuwait possible. They were sensitive to Saudi Arabia's expectation that the United States would quickly withdraw its forces from Saudi territory. The presence of a huge army of non-Muslims in a country that hosted Islam's holiest shrines was a real problem for Muslim leaders throughout the Middle East. Above all, Bush and his advisers wanted to maintain crucial support from Arab allies in the ongoing conflict with Iraq. With this support, and a continued US military presence in the Middle East, the administration believed it could contain Saddam Hussein and prevent any future Iraqi invasions.

No-Fly Zones

After the Republican Guard crushed the rebellions in Iraq, the United States decided to leave a remnant force in Saudi Arabia to enforce the cease-fire conditions. The military launched Operation Southern Watch, which established no-fly zones over southern and northern Iraq. The intent was to bar the Iraqi air forces from further airborne assaults on the Kurdish and Shiite rebel forces. A secondary goal, according to the cease-fire agreement, was to enforce inspections to ensure Iraq was now rid of its weapons of mass destruction. The British and French also kept a small contingent of military planes and trainers in the kingdom. Although many Saudi religious leaders objected to the presence of US, British, and French troops, the United States insisted on leaving these forces in place, pointing out they had been invited by the Saudi government to stay.

Iraq complied with inspections, up to a point. In 1998 UN inspectors were prevented from carrying out a search of Iraqi political offices that were suspected of housing hidden weapons. The Iraqis accused the United States and Britain of planting spies in the inspection teams in order to gather intelligence on Iraqi defenses. In December 1998 the US ambassador to the United Nations, Peter Burleigh, advised the inspection teams to withdraw for their own safety.

That same month the United States then carried out a four-day bombing campaign, code-named Operation Desert Fox. Air Force bombers, as well as Tomahawk cruise missiles fired from ships stationed in the Persian Gulf, damaged weapons manufacturing and research facilities, Republican Guard units, and the presidential palace. Although the United States declared the mission a success, Iraq ended any cooperation with the weapons inspection program. This action magnified the already-extreme distrust of Saddam Hussein by Western governments—and it would later be a major factor in the US invasion of Iraq in 2003.

A Defiant Iraqi Leader

The cease-fire and halt in military operations against Iraq left Saddam Hussein in power over a violently unstable nation. Revolts among the Kurds and Shiite opponents of the regime broke out—at the prompting of the United States—and were put down with great brutality. Saddam Hussein kept control over unconventional weapons, including chemical weapons, and could now claim to have survived an epic battle against a powerful military coalition. The Iraqi army remained a threat to Saudi Arabia and the global oil supply.

The confrontation between the United States and Iraq over the ban on weapons of mass destruction endured into the administration of George W. Bush, elected president in 2000. In the opinion of Bush and his advisers, Iraq had been interfering with weapons inspections since 1998. Iraq's refusal to comply with UN inspectors revealed, in their view, that Saddam Hussein must be defying the ban on weapons of mass destruction. The United States delivered ultimatums to Iraq through the UN, which—in a repeat of 1990—Saddam Hussein consistently defied.

The Trial of Saddam Hussein

Saddam Hussein survived the first Persian Gulf War but not the second. The conflict that broke out in 2003 swiftly ended the regime. After the invasion, however, the Iraqi leader fled Baghdad for the Sunni-dominated central provinces, which were friendly to his rule. After a chase lasting several months, he was finally captured by US troops near his hometown of Tikrit while hiding in a small underground chamber.

Although the United States had announced that bringing Saddam Hussein to justice was a primary goal of the war, the Americans handed him over to the new Iraqi government to settle the matter. In October 2005, the fugitive leader was brought before the Iraqi High Tribunal. Prosecutors reached back twenty-three years, to a mass shooting in the Shiite village of al-Dujayl—as well as other atrocities—to charge him with war crimes. In November 2006, the court pronounced Saddam Hussein guilty of murder, illegal imprisonment, and torture. A sentence of death was carried out on December 30.

The terrorist attack on September 11, 2001, was the turning point in this ongoing confrontation with Iraq. In an address to the nation on that day, President Bush announced, "I have directed the full resources of our intelligence and law enforcement communities to find those responsible and to bring them to justice. We will make no distinction between the terrorists who committed these acts and those who harbor them."[27]

Bush relied on reports that al Qaeda, the global terrorist network headed by Saudi businessman Osama bin Laden, was responsible for the attack. The Taliban government of Afghanistan had been providing shelter to al Qaeda and Bin Laden since the mid-1990s. Bush resolved to root out al Qaeda from Afghanistan and overthrow the Taliban regime. The United States accomplished this mission with an invasion of Afghanistan in the fall of 2001.

Bush then turned to Iraq and Saddam Hussein—in his view, an ongoing threat that his father and President Bill Clinton had not resolved. The United States returned to the United Nations with what it said was evidence that Iraq still harbored weapons of mass destruction. The United States also claimed that Iraq was protecting terrorist groups, including al Qaeda. But the Americans failed to obtain agreement on a UN resolution supporting military action against Iraq. Bush pressed ahead. He said he intended to defeat the threats of nuclear, chemical, and biological terrorism—even without a UN resolution. In March 2003, the United States staged a second invasion of southern Iraq.

Taking the Fight All the Way to Baghdad

This time, the United States brought the conflict all the way to Baghdad, resulting in the overthrow of the Iraqi government and the eventual capture and execution of Saddam Hussein. But the occupation of Iraq dragged on for years as an insurgency grew among Iraq's Sunni population and fighters recruited by an Iraqi branch of al Qaeda. In the meantime, UN weapons inspectors faulted the United States for reaching a convenient, foregone conclusion. Hans Blix, the UN head of this effort, declared that the Bush administration was simply looking for a pretext for invasion: "There were about

"There were about 700 inspections, and in no case did we find weapons of mass destruction."[28]

—Hans Blix, UN weapons inspector

Iraqi troops battle ISIS militants on the streets of Mosul, Iraq, in 2016. The terrorist group, which rose to power during the US invasion of Iraq in 2003, continues to commit brutal acts of terrorism in the Middle East and beyond.

700 inspections," he declared in an interview in 2004, "and in no case did we find weapons of mass destruction."[28]

The intention of the Second Persian Gulf War was to complete the work of the first. The survival of Saddam Hussein in 1991and the long confrontation between the United States and Iraq over the next twelve years were among its root causes. But the second president Bush could not muster the same level of international support for the effort, and the results were very different. The war dragged on for years, concluding with a retreat by the Americans, a civil war on the ground, and the rise of a new terrorist group known as the Islamic State in Iraq and Syria (ISIS), dedicated to establishing an Islamic caliphate (empire) in the Middle East.

After conquering large swaths of western Iraq and eastern Syria, ISIS brought its fight to Europe and threatened to infiltrate its members into the United States as well. The rise of ISIS, a group that occupies little territory but draws recruits from around the world over the Internet, was one of the most important legacies of the Second Persian Gulf War. With a range and effectiveness even greater than al Qaeda, ISIS is challenging military strategists to develop an entirely new approach to warfare and maintaining the violent turmoil that has endured for centuries in the Middle East.

Introduction: Freedom, War, and Oil

1. Quoted in *Sun Sentinel*, "Memorable Quotes Echoing from 1991." http://articles.sun-sentinel.com.
2. Quoted in American Presidency Project, "George Bush: Address Before a Joint Session of the Congress on the State of the Union, January 29, 1991." www.presidency.ucsb.edu.
3. Quoted in James A. Warren, "The Gulf War Victory That Never Was," Daily Beast, February 20, 2016. www.thedailybeast.com.

Chapter 1: A Brief History of the Persian Gulf War

4. Quoted in Jon Meacham, *Destiny and Power: The American Odyssey of George Herbert Walker Bush*. New York: Random House, 2015, pp. 432–33.
5. Quoted in *Frontline*, "Oral History: Margaret Thatcher," PBS. www.pbs.org.
6. Quoted in John F. Burns, "Confrontation in the Gulf: From an Old Iraqi Battlefield, Warnings of New Bloodshed," *New York Times*, September 29, 1990. www.nytimes.com.
7. Quoted in Gordon Furr's Home Page, "Excerpts from Iraqi Document on Meeting with US Envoy," Montclair State University. https://msuweb.montclair.edu/~furrg.
8. Quoted in Lawrence Freedman and Efraim Karsh, *The Gulf Conflict, 1990–1991*. Princeton, NJ: Princeton University Press, 1995, p. 363.
9. Quoted in American Presidency Project, "The President's News Conference on the Persian Gulf Conflict," March 1, 1991. www.presidency.ucsb.edu.
10. Quoted in Freedman and Karsh, *The Gulf Conflict, 1990–1991*, p. 410.

Chapter 2: How Did Oil Politics Fuel the Gulf War?

11. Quoted in NPR, "The 1973 Arab Oil Embargo: The Old Rules No Longer Apply," *Parallels* (blog). www.npr.org.
12. Quoted in Thomas C. Hayes, "Confrontation in the Gulf," *New York Times*, September 3, 1990. www.nytimes.com.

13. Quoted in Gordon Furr's Home Page, "Excerpts from Iraqi Document on Meeting with U.S. Envoy."
14. Quoted in Paul Aarts and Michael Renner, "Oil and the Gulf War," Middle East Research and Information Project. www.merip.org.
15. Quoted in *Frontline*, "Oral History: Colin Powell," PBS. www.pbs.org.

Chapter 3: How Did the Cold War's End Influence the Persian Gulf Conflict?

16. Quoted in Alan Cowell, "War in the Gulf: Jordan; Jordanian Ends Neutrality, Assailing Allied War Effort," *New York Times*, February 7, 1991. www.nytimes.com.
17. Quoted in Freedman and Karsh, *The Gulf Conflict, 1990–1991*, p. 163.
18. Quoted in Michael R. Gordon, "Hussein Wanted Soviets to Head Off U.S. in 1991," *New York Times*, January 19, 2011. www.nytimes.com.

Chapter 4: What Was the Result of Basing US and Coalition Troops in Saudi Arabia?

19. Quoted in Charles Kurzman, "Pro-US Fatwas," Middle East Policy Council. www.mepc.org.
20. Quoted in Lawrence Wright, *The Looming Tower: Al Qaeda and the Road to 9/11*. New York: Alfred A. Knopf, 2006, p. 187.
21. Quoted in Alan Greenblatt, "Twenty Years Later, the First Iraq War Still Resonates," NPR. www.npr.org.
22. Quoted in Combating Terrorism Center, "Letters from Bin Laden," West Point. www.ctc.usma.edu.
23. Quoted in Yossef Bodansky, *Bin Laden: The Man Who Declared War on America*. Roseville, CA: Prima, 1999, p. 190.

Chapter 5: What Resulted from Allowing Saddam Hussein to Remain in Power?

24. Quoted in Freedman and Karsh, *The Gulf Conflict, 1990–1991*, pp. 163, 404.
25. Quoted in Military Officers Association of America, "Colin Powell Remembers Desert Storm." www.moaa.org.

26. Quoted in *New York Times*, "War in the Gulf: Bush Statement," February 16, 1991. www.nytimes.com.
27. Quoted in American Rhetoric, "George Bush: 9/11 Address to the Nation." www.americanrhetoric.com.
28. Quoted in Bonnie Azab Powell, "UN Weapons Inspector Hans Blix Faults Bush Administration for Lack of 'Critical Thinking' in Iraq," UC Berkeley News. www.berkeley.edu.

Books

William Thomas Allison, *The Gulf War, 1990–1991*. New York: Palgrave Macmillan, 2012.

Dexter Filkins, *The Forever War*. New York: Vintage, 2009.

Colin Powell, *My American Journey*. New York: Ballantine, 2003.

H. Norman Schwarzkopf, *It Doesn't Take a Hero: The Autobiography*. New York: Bantam, 1993.

Anthony Tucker-Jones, *The Gulf War: Operation Desert Storm, 1990–1991*. South Yorkshire, UK: Pen and Sword, 2014.

Daniel Yergin, *The Prize: The Epic Quest for Oil, Money and Power*. New York: Free Press, 2008.

Internet Sources

Center of Military History, *War in the Persian Gulf: Operations Desert Shield and Desert Storm, August 1990–March 1991*. www.history.army.mil/html/books/070/70-117-1/CMH_70-117-1.pdf.

Frontline, "Oral History: Colin Powell," PBS. www.pbs.org/wgbh/pages/frontline/gulf/oral/powell/1.html.

History.com, "Osama bin Laden." www.history.com/topics/osama-bin-laden.

Middle East Research and Information Project, "Oil and the Gulf War." www.merip.org/mer/mer171/oil-gulf-war.

Edward Mortimer, "Iraq: The Road Not Taken," *New York Review of Books*. www.nybooks.com/articles/1991/05/16/iraq-the-road-not-taken.

Office of the Historian, "The First Gulf War," US Department of State. https://history.state.gov/departmenthistory/short-history/firstgulf.

Stratfor, "Geopolitics of the Northwestern Persian Gulf." www.strat for.com/video/geopolitics-northwestern-persian-gulf.

Kate Zernike and Michael T. Kaufman, "The Most Wanted Face of Terrorism," *New York Times*. www.nytimes.com/2011/05/02/world /02osama-bin-laden-obituary.html.

Websites

Army Live, "A Timeline of Operation Desert Storm" (http://army live.dodlive.mil/index.php/2013/02/operation-desert-storm). This web-page, which is part of the US Army's official blog, posts a day-to-day time line of the war, with many concise and useful details on the war in the air and on the ground.

The Gulf War (www.pbs.org/wgbh/pages/frontline/gulf/). Designed to offer in-depth coverage of the war based on PBS's two-part *Front-line* documentary series, with an introduction, video clips, maps, oral histories, chronologies, and episode transcripts.

Office of the Historian (https://history.state.gov). A US State De-partment website with documents and articles on the Persian Gulf War, with an emphasis on the diplomatic efforts made by the Bush administration to turn back the invasion of Kuwait.

Persian Gulf War (www.history.com/topics/persian-gulf-war). An excellent summary of the Persian Gulf conflict by the History Chan-nel, with a collection of videos, speeches, and audio clips offering in-sight into the war's background and main events.

forces in Saudi Arabia, 47, 48
freedom and liberty as reasons
given, 32–33
soldiers, **10**
Soviet Union cooperation with, 37,
41, 42, 44
threat to oil and, 31–33
warning from Saddam Hussein to,
30–31
weaponry, 19
rebellions in Iraq and, 62, 63–64
Taliban in Afghanistan and, 54, 66
terrorism against
Bin Laden's first attacks on
Americans and, 53

car bombings of US embassies in
Africa and, 54
and retaliation against terrorists, 54
September 11, 2001, attacks and,
11, 53, 54–56, **55**, 66

Vietnam War
absence of coalition during, 23
media coverage of, 17
syndrome, 16
Vietnam syndrome as result of, 8, 11

Warbah island, 27, 28
weapons of mass destruction, 64, 66
women and Islam, 52, 54

Tom Streissguth has written more than one hundred nonfiction books for the school and library market. A graduate of Yale University, he has worked as a teacher, editor, and journalist and has traveled through Europe, the Middle East, and Southeast Asia. He currently lives in Woodbury, Minnesota, where he founded The Archive, a publishing company specializing in the work of historic American journalists.

Christian Jr./Sr High School
2100 Greenfield Dr.
El Cajon, CA 92019